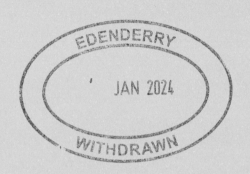

A World of Field Trips

Going to a Beach

Rebecca Rissman

www.raintreepublishers.co.uk
Visit our website to find out more information about Raintree books.

To order:
☎ Phone 0845 6044371
📄 Fax +44 (0) 1865 312263
✉ Email myorders@raintreepublishers.co.uk

Customers from outside the UK please telephone +44 1865 312262

Raintree is an imprint of Capstone Global Library Limited, a company incorporated in England and Wales having its registered office at 7 Pilgrim Street, London, EC4V 6LB – Registered company number: 6695582.

Edited by Rebecca Rissman, Dan Nunn, and Catherine Veitch
Designed by Richard Parker
Picture research by Tracy Cummins
Originated by Capstone Global Library Ltd
Printed and bound in China by Leo Paper Products Ltd

ISBN 978 1 406 23515 9
16 15 14 13 12 11
10 9 8 7 6 5 4 3 2 1

British Library Cataloguing in Publication Data
Rissman, Rebecca.
Going to a beach. -- (World of field trips)
551.4'57-dc22

Acknowledgements
We would like to thank the following for permission to reproduce photographs: Corbis pp. 16 (© TWPhoto), 17 (© John Stanmeyer/VII), 20 (© moodboard); Getty Images pp. 5 (Hans Neleman), 15 (Darren Robb), 18 (Macduff Everton), 21 (Coto Elizondo); istockphoto pp. 4 (© Sean Locke), 6 (© David Cannings- Bushell), 9 (© ra-photos), 10 (© Jay Spooner), 23d (© ra-photos); Shutterstock pp. 7 (© Vinicius Tupinamba), 8 left (© Dominik Michálek), 8 right (© Cees Nooij), 11 (© BlueOrange Studio), 12 (© Joyce Marrero), 13 (© Connie Lanyon-Roberts), 14 (© oliveromg), 19 (© Yuri Arcurs), 22 (© Jan Kranendonk), 23a (© Cees Nooij), 23b (© oliveromg), 23c (© Dominik Michálek).

Front cover photograph of children running on a beach reproduced with permission of Photolibrary (Denis Debadier/ Photononstop). Back cover photograph of a rocky beach reproduced with permission of Shutterstock (© Joyce Marrero).

Every effort has been made to contact copyright holders of any material reproduced in this book. Any omissions will be rectified in subsequent printings if notice is given to the publisher.

Contents

Field trips

People go on field trips to visit new places.

People go on field trips to learn
new things.

Field trip to a beach

Some people go on field trips to beaches.

beach

A beach is near the water.

pebbles

sand

Some beaches are covered in pebbles. Some beaches are covered in sand.

Most sand is made of tiny pieces
of rocks and shells.

Different beaches

This beach has black sand.

The sand gets hot in the sun!

This beach is rocky.

The waves crash against the rocks.

Be careful!

This beach has sand dunes.

sand dune

You can climb up the sand dunes.

This beach is made by humans.

The people put sand here for you to enjoy.

This beach has white sand.

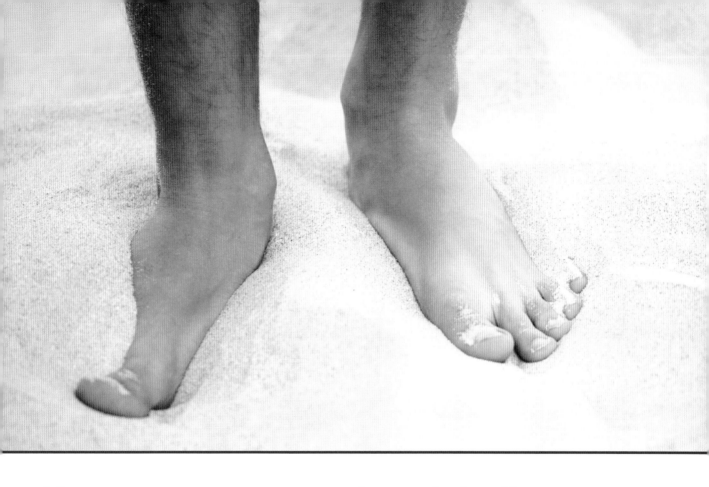

You can press your toes into the warm sand.

How should you behave at the beach?

Always wear suncream at the beach.

Only swim when adults are nearby.

What do you think?

What kind of beach is this?

Look on page 24 for the answer.

Picture glossary

 **beach** area of land near lakes, oceans, or seas. A beach can be sandy or rocky.

 **dune** hill of sand. Sand dunes can be very large.

 **pebble** small rock

 **sand** tiny pieces of rock and shells that can be found on beaches

Index

Notes for parents and teachers

Before reading

Explain to children that a field trip is a short visit to a new place, and that it often takes place during a school day. Ask children if they have ever taken a field trip. Show children the front cover of the book and ask them if they know what landform the cover shows. Explain to them that it is a beach, and that beaches are the areas of land near water. Some beaches are covered in pebbles, while others are covered in sand.

After reading

- Show children the images on pages 10–11, and then compare them with the images on pages 18–19. Explain to children that the sand is different colours because it is made of different materials. The black sand beach comes from black volcanic rock. The white sand comes from light-coloured shells and stones.

- Remind children to practise good water safety when they are at the beach. Have children brainstorm a list of good safety tips, and make a "Beach Safety" poster to hang in the classroom. Remember to include items such as only swimming when adults are near.

Answer to page 22

It is a pebble beach.